... not just a SLAVE!

D1368684

Written by Angeline Dean
Illustrations by Christina O.

Dedication

First and Foremost, I thank the God of Abraham, Isaac, and Jacob for His strength in finishing the project! I dedicate this book to my best friend and #1 girl-my grandmother, the late Mary V. Dean-Dillard. Margaret Suess-Harris, my other grandmother, who was always there supporting me. To my parents-Dr's Frederick & Eveline Dean- my father who especially planted a seed in my life at young age. As "my punishment" I had to read the Black Encyclopedia. He stated, "Read the stuff they will never teach you in school." To my uncle Keith Dillard-THANK YOU for being more of a big brother than an uncle! THANK YOU for teaching me firsthand what to watch out for while going through my "girly" times. To my niece Ny'Aira Dean, who took the time to become more knowledgeable concerning her history. To every young person who participated in my focus groups. To Professor Ron Covil, Alexandra Fields, Chris Gazzara, and Professor V. To every Pastor, Apostle, Evangelist, Prophet and Prophetess who has sowed into my life-THANK YOU! Rev. Dorothy Lutes, Monica Bell, and Apostle DeeAnn Waite-I am waiting for companies and books to come to fruition- tag you're next! To a host of Cousins, Family, Friends and my "children" and God children-I pray that you will learn the fullness of ALL that you are! To Christina O and Victoria Birch for your dedication and professionalism. To Michelle Thomas, my business partner who is my African American guru. For everyone who didn't believe in me-MUCH THANKS!

Special thanks to Chike Akua, Stacie Smith of Detroit, and RATHSI Publishing for their inspiration and motivation.

Preface

I especially thank my cousin, Aryka Thomas who was the inspiration behind the book. Her question, "Am I Just a Slave" not only saddened me, but also angered me. But more importantly, it provoked me to write this book. To every child whose schools start off teaching and re-emphasizing slavery—KNOW YOU COME FROM GREATNESS, AND YOU ARE NOT A SLAVE AT ALL!!

WWW.RATHSIPUBLISHING.COM
(516) 224-7464
INFO@RATHSIPUBLISHING.COM

ATTENTION CORPORATIONS, UNIVERSITIES, COLLEGES, AND PROFESSIONAL ORGANIZATIONS: Quantity discounts are available on bulk purchases of this book for educational, gift purposes, or as premiums for increasing magazine subscriptions or renewals. Special books or book excerpts can also be created to fit specific needs. For information, please contact:

Angeline Dean
ang1dean@yahoo.com
(609) 284-2839
ISBN: 978-1-936937-29-5
Printed in the United States of America.

AFONSO I- King of the Kongo 1506-1540 (or 1543)

We cannot reckon how great the damage is, since the merchants daily seize our subjects, sons of the land and sons of our noblemen, vassals and relatives ... and cause them to be sold; and so great, Sir, is their corruption and licentiousness that our country is being utterly depopulated.

—Afonso I, in a letter to King João of Portugal, 1526

Afonso I was the first ruler to resist the most despicable act ever known to man-the European slave trade. Afonso was a Christian King of Kongo (now known as the Democratic republic of the Congo) and was the first to ever attempt to Europeanize the kingdom of Africa. Afonso ruled for thirty-seven years-the longest reign in the history of the Kongo. His vision was to unify his nation, fully equipping it with advanced knowledge and technology. While reigning, he started building churches and declared Catholicism the official state religion. Partnerships with the kings of Portugal were established. These kings of Portugal had previously sent explorers and traders to the Kongo since the 1480's.

Afonso's son, Henrique became a bishop in the Roman Catholic Church in 1518. This position further strengthened the ties between the Kongo and Portugal. King Afonso I controlled the trade himself. This revenue was based primarily upon the trading of ivory and raffia fabric; it was supplemented by trade tolls and taxes.

Although Afonso I wanted technical aid from Portuguese to provide his people with technical skills and education from Europe, the Portuguese, unfortunately, were predominantly interested in the slave trade. From 1514, the slave trade became a vital part of the economy, and Africans were brutalized and dehumanized. This portion of the economy provided the financing of the priests, artisans, and teachers, as well as purchased noble items for them.

...not just a *SLAVE!*

BEHANZIN HOSSU BOWELLE- The King of the Shark (1841-1906)

Behanzin was the most powerful ruler known to West Africa at the end of the nineteenth century. His army was strong, powerful, and physically fit. It consisted of a division of 5000 females, and some of the most dreaded, superior warriors. These females and superior warriors, along with the rest of the army resisted European interventions at all costs.

During his reign, the French were determined to annex Dahomey. Behanzin and his family refused adamantly to sign a treaty. Eventually, Dahomey became a French colony. This was one of the best-organized independent states of West Africa, and was one of the last African kingdoms yielding to the European colonialist. Behanzin was exiled to the island of Martinique in the West Indies, and later transferred to Algeria, where in 1906, he died.

The King Shark, which Behanzin was often referred to, was a Dahomeyan surname that symbolized strength and wisdom. He is also credited with some of the finest songs and poetry created and produced in Dahomey.

...not just a *SLAVE!*

HANNIBAL- Ruler of Carthage (247-183 B.C.)

Hannibal was known as the greatest general and militant strategist who ever lived. He succeeded his father at the age of twenty-six as commander of armies. He used his overpowering African armies to conquer major portions of Spain and Italy. Hannibal is known for causing Rome to lose a million men due to war and destroyed bridges and cities.

Hannibal marched his army with trained African War elephants through the treacherous Alps to surprise and conquer northern Italy. He mobilized between 60,000-100,000 troops. This task at the very least was daunting; as both had to be provisioned along the way. His tactical genius earned him recognition that has spanned more than 2000 years.

Hannibal also served as a non-royal magistrate and was granted control over a city-state.

Today, the military tactics of Hannibal are still being studied in numerous military schools.

...not just a *SLAVE!*

IMHOTEP- The World's First known Genius

Imhotep, whose name translates as 'Prince of Peace" was born in Ankhtowe, a suburb of Memphis, Egypt.

He was born on May 31, and although the year is not quite definite, it is recorded that he was the royal advisor to King Zoser during the third Dynasty of Kemet. He is regarded as the world's first recorded multi-genius-he was an architect, astronomer, philosopher, poet and physician.

As an architect, the Step Pyramid at Sakkara is the only of his achievements that can still be seen and appreciated today. This pyramid is the first structure ever built of cut stone; it is the oldest of the Seven Wonders of the World. Although it took about twenty years to complete, it was not considered a very long time considering the newness of the idea. During this period (between 3000B.C.E. and 1100 C.E.), bronze, amongst other metals were used for the very first time.

Imhotep was given a host of titles during his lifetime. He was known as The Chancellor of the King of Lower Kemet, The First after the King of Upper Kemet, High Priest of Heliopolis and administrator of The Great Palace.

While serving as a physician, it is Imhotep who is believed to have authored more than ninety (90) anatomical terms and forty-eight (48) injuries. This occurred well over two thousand two hundred (2,200) years before the Western Father of Medicine, Hippocrates, was born.

As a philosopher and poet, Imhotep's most remembered phrase is "Eat, drink, and be merry for tomorrow we shall die."

...not just a *SLAVE!*

KHAMA- The Good King of Bechuanaland (1819-1923)

Khama's reign is distinguished by his being a highly regarded, peace loving ruler. He possessed a desire and ability to extract technological innovations from Europeans; yet, he resisted their attempts to colonize his country. Khama's advancements include the building of schools, scientific cattle feeding, and the introduction of a mounted police corps. His institution of cattle feeding greatly improved his countries prestige and wealth. During his reign, all forms of crime were known to be as low as zero.

Respect for Khama was so exemplified that during a visit with Queen Victoria of England, he protested English settlement in Bechuanaland in 1875. The English honored Khama and validated his appeal for the continued freedom for Bechuanaland.

...not just a *SLAVE!*

MENELEK II – King of Kings of Abyssinia (1844-1913)

Menelek was proclaimed to be a descendant of the legendary Queen of Sheba and King Solomon. He was known as the overshadowing figure of his time in Africa. He united many independent kingdoms into the strong stable empire known as the United States of Abyssinia (Ethiopia). This feat consisted of several kingdoms, which often fiercely opposed each other. For conquering this feat, Menelek is known as one of the greatest statesman of African history. His further accomplishments in dealing with world powers on the international scene, coupled with the 1896 victory over Italy in the Battle of Adwa, an attempt to invade his country, catapulted him amongst the great leaders of world history and maintained his country's independence until 1935.

...not just a *SLAVE!*

NARMER –Founder of Dynastic Kemet (3200 B.C.)

The Greeks knew Narmer, or Aha as Menes. He is regarded as the founder of Dynastic Kemet. He is responsible for leading an army from Upper Kemet (which was in the South) to conquer Lower Kemet (which was located in the North) around 3200 B.C. He then united the Upper and Lower Kemet in to one nation upon which thirty (30) dynasties would follow. During this time hieroglyphic writing or any other type of writing in the world would make its appearance.

Building a city on his newly conquered land was one of Narmer's first tasks. It was here that he was incumbered with such a monumental task- the Delta region was covered with an immense swamp. In order to rectify his situation, Narmer drained the swamp that actually diverted the course of the Nile River. A city called Men-Nefer (A Good Place), was built on this new land. Men-Nefer served as the capital of Kemet for several centuries.

It is slated that an Arab traveler would refer to the city as "stretching a days journey in every direction." This writing was recorded as late as the middle ages. The Greeks later renamed Men-Nefer "Memphis" a name that today still honors a King who existed nearly five thousand (5000) years ago.

...not just a *SLAVE!*

JAJA- King of the Opobo (1821-1891)

Jubo Jubogha was forced into slavery at the age of twelve. He obtained his freedom while still young, and became an independent, prosperous trader. He became the chief of his people as well as the head of his Eastern Nigerian City State of Bonny.

Opobo was an area near the Eastern Nigeria River and was established by JaJa. Here he became king. This area was very popular as it was also a favorable trading route. It soon attracted attention from the greedy Europeans whose main goal was to capture this trading route. JaJa was known to fiercely resist this intervention until finally, he was captured by the British at age seventy, and placed into exile to the West Indies. Unfortunately, this great nineteenth century Ibo leader never saw his kingdom again.

...not just a *SLAVE!*

KHUFU –The Father of Pyramid Building (2551-2528)

Known also by the Greek name "Cheops," King Khufu was the father of pyramid building at Giza. Khufu was a young King who came to the throne in his twenties.

Beginning in the year two thousand, several inscriptional pieces of evidence has been found on pyramids proving his existence as well as this pyramid. Some of this inscription also proved that Khufu likely led military expeditions into the Sinai, Nubia, and Libya.

In addition to the splendor of this Great Pyramid which stood four hundred eighty one feet tall, an ancient wooden huge boat was found sealed in a pit at the base of this Great Pyramid.

...not just a *SLAVE!*

MANSA KANHAN MUSSA – King of Mali (1306-1332)

This king was a great economist, a scholar, a true man of the arts, and an accomplished businessman. He is well known for the impact he created due to his flamboyant style.

In 1324, this King of Mali led his people on the Hadj- a holy pilgrimage from Timbuktu to Mecca. He safely led a caravan of seventy two thousand people across the Sahara Desert and back; a total distance of six thousand four hundred ninety six miles. This event was so spectacular, that Mansa Kanhan Mussa ascertained the respect of scholars and traders throughout the entire world.

The region of Mali during his reign was not only one of the most prestigious and wealthiest empires in the world, but also was the home of one of the worlds most prestigious universities in Timbuktu.

...not just a *SLAVE!*

SHAKA – King of the Zulus (1818-1828)

Shaka was recognized as a strong leader and military innovator; yet, he is noted for revolutionizing the nineteenth century Bantu warfare. His military genius was evidenced as he first grouped his regiments by their age. He then trained his men to use basic, standardized weapons along with special tactics. He developed what is known as an "assegai," a short stabbing spear. This weapon was used along with a tight formation of his men, and large shields to fend off the enemies throwing spears.

Shaka's troops earned such a reputation over the years that enemies would flee at the sight of them.

Shaka united a powerful nation by uniting all tribes in South Africa. This nation consisted of more than one million people who fought against the despicable traces of colonial rule.

...not just a *SLAVE!*

MOSHOESHOL – King of Basutoland (1815 – 1868)

Moshoeshol was known to be wise, just, and as brilliant in the skill of diplomacy as he was brilliant in battle. Law and order prevailed as he united many diverse groups of people into a stable society where they could nurse their crops and cattle in peace. He was a skillful negotiator, often avoided conflict, and understood the concept that peace bought about prosperity.

...not just a *SLAVE!*

MUTATO –The Greatest Mutato (1440)

In 1440, King Mutato and his council understood that as long as even their most advanced states stood independent and alone, they would be doomed by criminal exploits from the Europeans. It was imperative that they unify into a single nation and possess a strong central government. Mutato and his men set forward to carry out this campaign of uniting Africans into a sphere that cut across South Africa, and covered Zimbabwe with an infinite boundary that spread beyond the Zambezi River in Zambia. It went over Mozambique to the Indian Ocean, and swept southward to reposses the entire coastline fronting the New Empire. It is here that the majority of the world's precious metals such as gold, copper, tin, and iron were held in over four thousand mines. Unity was finally achieved in 1480 after thirty years of struggle; thus, the Empire of Monomotapa.

...not just a *SLAVE!*

OSEI TUTU- King of Asante (1680 –1717)

Osei Tutu was the founder and first King of the Asante nation. Ghana now rests where this great West African forest kingdom resided. Osei Tutu persuaded and united over six different nations under his leadership. Under his reign, the geographic area of Asante tripled in size, gold was the prime source of wealth, and the kingdom became significant in power. His military and political prowess has now endured for two centuries.

...not just a *SLAVE!*

TAHARQA/TAHARKA – King of the Nubia (710-664 B.C.)

Taharka is said to be one of the most famous rulers of Napatan Kush. He was heir to a kingdom that included not only Kush but also Kemet. At the age of thirty-two, he became king. Yet at the age of sixteen, this amazing Nubian King led armies against the invading Assyrians in defense of his ally, Israel. These great expeditions are mentioned in the Bible (Isaiah 37:9; 2 Kings 19:9).

Taharka is also said to have once commanded military campaigns in Western Asia as far away as Palestine and led expeditions all the way to Spain. Taharka led a twenty-five year reign during which he controlled the largest empire in Ancient Africa. Only the Assyrians equaled him in power. Although these two forces were in constant conflict, Taharka managed to initiate a building program throughout his empire that was gigantic in scope. Both the majesty and numbers of his building projects were legendary, with the greatest being the temple at Gebel Barkal in Sudan.

This temple is decorated with images of Taharka over one hundred feet high and was carved from the living rock.

...not just a *SLAVE!*

TENKAMENIN – King of Ghana (1037-1075)

During the reign of Tenkamenin, the country of Ghana ascertained its greatness. Tenkamenin's empire flourished economically due to his careful and strategic management of the gold trade across the Sahara desert into West Africa. His greatest strengths however, were in government. Tenkamenin would daily ride out on horseback to listen to the concerns and problems of his people. He insisted that no one be denied an audience. They were allowed to remain in his presence until they were satisfied that justice was served. He is considered one of the greatest models of African rule due to his religious tolerance and his democratic monarchy principles.

...not just a *SLAVE!*

THUTMOSE III – Pharaoh of Egypt (1504 – 1450 B.C.)

Thutmose III was a member of one of the greatest families in the history of African royalty. His family laid the foundation of the eighteenth Dynasty of ancient Egypt.

Thutmose III was angry and frustrated for a great portion of his life due to the fact that his sister Hatshepsut came to power before he did. Ironically, however, it was the assignments given to him by Hatshepsut that proved to not only aid in his rise to power, but also aided him in gleaning the responsibilities necessary of his royal position.

After overcoming his anger issues, Thutmose goes on to become one of the most important Pharaohs in Egyptian history. He is credited as a great warrior who strengthened the sovereignty of Kemet and extended its influence into Western Asia.

...not just a *SLAVE!*

SAMORY TOURE – The Black Napoleon of the Sudan (1830 – 1900)

Samory Toure's ascendance began when his native Bissandugu was attacked and his mother was taken captive. Samory persuades his attackers to take him instead of his mother. His petition was granted, but later he escaped and joined the army of King Bitike Souane of Torona. Due to a quick rise in Bitike's army, Samory returned to Bissandugu where he was quickly installed as king.   In this position, he defied the wicked exploits of the French in Africa by launching a quest to unify West Africa as a single state. After eighteen years of conflict with France, Samory Toure not only continued to frustrate the Europeans with his military strategy and tactics, but also earned the African monarch title: "The Black Napoleon of the Sudan" from some of France's greatest commanders.

...not just a *SLAVE!*

AMINA-Queen of Zaria (1588-1589)

Amina was the queen of Zazzua, which is a province of Nigeria-now known as Zaria. She was born around 1533 and thought to be the granddaughter of King Sarkin of Zazzau Nohir. Zazzua was one of a number of city-states that dominated the trans-Saharan trade centers. It was known to trade mainly leather items, salt, cloth, kola, horses, and imported metals; this town was very wealthy.

At the age of sixteen, Amina became the apparent heir to her mother, Bakwa, the ruling queen of Zazzua. Because of this title, Amina was responsible for a ward in the city and daily councils with other officials. Amina decided to learn military skills from the warriors, although her mother was known for peace and prosperity. This was a decision that paid off for her in the end. Around 1566, queen Bakwa died and the reign of Zazzua was passed to Amina's younger brother Karma. During his reign, Amina became known as the leading warrior of the Zazzua Cavalry and her military tactics and achievements brought her great wealth and great power. Karma died after reigning for ten years and Amina now became the queen of Zazzua. Amina reigned for thirty-four years where she expanded the domain of Zazzua to its largest size ever, created safe passages for traders, and enforced defensive walls around military camps. Many of these towns are still in existence today due to their growth because of the protective walls. Amina is mostly remembered as "a woman as capable as a man."

...not just a *SLAVE!*

CANDACE- Empress of Ethiopia (332 B.C.)

Candace was known as one of the greatest generals of the ancient world. She was a **world famous military tactician and field commander.** It has been said that Alexander reached Kemet (known as Ancient Egypt) around 333 B.C. on one of his world conquering rampages, but bought his army to a halt as it reached the borders of Ethiopia. Alexander did not want to have his world famous reputation and his chain of victories tainted by risking a defeat by a woman. He knew that there were awaiting black armies with Queen Candace in personal command at those borders.

Candace is also an Ethiopian queen mentioned in the Bible. She was so wealthy that she had an Ethiopian eunuch in charge of her treasury. (Acts 8:26-28)

...not just a SLAVE!

CLEOPATRA VII- Queen of Kemet (Ancient Egypt-the land of the Blacks) 69-30 B.C.

To this day, Cleopatra is still deliberately portrayed as a white woman, yet she is known to be of African descent (possibly African/Greek). Cleopatra came to power at the age of seventeen and is the most popular of the seven queens carrying this name. Cleopatra was known to have mastered many different languages and several African dialects. She became highly instrumental in reaching beyond the border of Egypt and was extremely instrumental in making Kemet (Egypt) in to the world number one super power at that time.

Cleopatra strove hard to turn Egypt into a world supremacy and enlisted the military services of two great Roman leaders. She first persuaded Julius Caesar, and later Mark Anthony to renounce their allegiances in order to fight on behalf of Egypt. Before Cleopatra's dreams of a conquest were established, both men met their deaths. Cleopatra was so disheartened and depressed that she pressed an asp (snake) to her breast and ended her life.

...not just a *SLAVE!*

HATSHEPSUT- Queen of Kemet (Ancient Egypt the land of the Blacks) 1503-1482 B. C.

Hatshepsut was known as "The Ablest Queen of Far Antiquity" and held this title for thiry-three years. Although known as a "warrior" queen, initially she found herself predominantly fighting for the position of power and respect in the Kemetic hierarchy. Hatshepsut would often dress in masculine attire and entertained a beard in order to gain respect.

Before becoming a ruler, Hatshepsut actively advocated for things known to be of importance to all African leaders: the expansion of foreign trade, perfection of national defense, international diplomatic relations, vast public building programs, and securing the South and the North through either peace or war. One of her "pet projects" however, was building a great navy for both commerce and war. She also had a number of temples and pyramids erected in order to enhance her popularity with the Egyptian people.

Hatshepsut rose to power after her father Thothmes I was stricken with paralysis. He appointed his daughter as his chief aide and heiress to the throne. Due to her success on the throne and in many of the facets she served, she became known as one of the giants of the race.

...not just a *SLAVE!*

MAKEDA-QUEEN OF SHEBA (The Symbol of Beauty) 960 B.C.

Makeda, Queen of Sheba, was one of the great Queens of Ethiopia. Many argue that she was not black, but this beautiful queen is mentioned in the Bible (1Kings 10 and 2 Chronicles 9). Upon studying, you will see where she is from. Ethiopia was South of Egypt and bordered the west bank of the Red Sea. Ethiopia also embraced regions east of the Red Sea to include territories known today a Saudi Arabia and Yemen. During these times, Ethiopia was second only to Egypt in power and fame.

King Solomon was so captivated by the beauty of the Ethiopians, as well as their history, spiritual traditions and their wealth. Makeda learned of the wealth of King Solomon through a wealthy merchant by the name of Tamerin. She was so intrigued that she visited. She knew her visit would incur a significant ceremonial affair as was the custom of royal visits at this time. Therefore, she bought with her 120 talents of gold, an abundance of spices, and precious stones. She traveled the Sahara Desert with more than 797 camels and donkeys too numerous to mention. The value of the gold this beautiful queen gave King Solomon was valued at $3,690,000 dollars.

King Solomon was so enamored with this queen, that he made sure she had the best of food, elaborate banquets, numerous changes of garments, and silken carpets adorned with fringes of gold, silver, diamonds and pearls. He had his choice of any woman and fell in love with this beautiful black queen.

It is said that he fathered a son by the name of Menelik by her.

...not just a *SLAVE!*

NANDI-Queen of Zululand (1778-1826 A.D.)

In the year of 1786 the King of Zululand was overjoyed and ecstatic! His wife, Nandi, had just given birth to a beautiful baby boy-the King's first son. Soon afterwards, the King's other wives became very jealous, envious, and bitter and pressured the King to banish Nandi and their son into exile.

Nandi was a proud woman and she raised her son by giving him all of the kinds of trainings and guidance of a royal heir. She sacrificed much, but was openly rewarded when her son Shaka returned to Zululand and became the greatest of all Zulu Kings.

She is, to this day still revered as "Nandi- a woman of high esteem." She did not let her early days of being exiled stop her from accomplishing great things.

...not just a *SLAVE!*

NEFERTITI- Nubian Queen of Kemet (Ancient Egypt the land of the Blacks) 1292-1225

Nefertiti is considered on of the most beautiful women in the world. Her marriage to Akhenaten, the originator of the one god concept (monotheism) was known as one of the greatest known love affairs in history. This marriage also brought the hundred years of war between Nubia and Egypt to an end.

Nefertiti is known to have participated in all of the religious ceremonies with her husband; thus thrusting her into an active role in the reshaping of herself in civilization. Akhenaten is known for affording his chief wife substantial authority, which was known to be unprecedented in Egyptian history. Today, monuments still stand in Queen Nefertiti's honor. The temple that was built for her at Abu Simbel is one of the largest and most beautiful structures ever built to honor a wife, as well as celebrate peace.

...not just a *SLAVE!*

NEHANDA-(Mbuya-grandmother) of Zimbabwe

Nehanda was born into a religious family and became one of Zimbabwe's most influential religious leaders. Nehanda is known to have displayed impeccable organizational and leadership skills at a young age.

In 1896, English settlers invaded Zimbabwe and began to confiscate the land and the cattle. Nehanda and other leaders declared an all out war. At first they maintained great success, but soon supplies began to shorten. Because of this, the victories became slim and Nehanda was captured and found guilty. She was then executed for the ordering of the death of a notorious cruel native commander. Although Nehanda has been deceased for nearly a hundred years, she is still known, referred and respected as Mbuya (grandmother) Nehanda by Zimbabwean patriots.

...not just a *SLAVE!*

NZINGHA-Amazon Queen of Matamba, West Africa (1582-1663)

This Angolan queen was known as a symbol of inspiration everywhere and ranked among the great rulers of Africa. She was an excellent military leader as well as an astute diplomat. Nzingha waged war against the savage slave-hunting Europeans that lasted nearly thirty years, and was even sent to negotiate peace with the Portuguese when the army of her brothers' kingdom was attacked. After this, she formed her own army against the Portuguese.

Nzingha was a self-sacrificing, competent, political leader and was wholeheartedly devoted to the resistance movement. Her battles reached colossal history as she allied her nation with the Dutch, thus forming the first African European alliance against a European oppressor. Nzingha is said to have possessed both masculine hardness and a feminine charm, in which she portrayed both. She used religion as a political tool whenever the situation suited.

Nandi, the mother of the great King Shaka Zulu, is said to have mounted offense against invaders due to the following of Nzingha.

...not just a *SLAVE!*

TIYE-The Nubian Queen of Kemet (Ancient Egypt) 1415-1340 B.C.

Queen Tiye is regarded as one of the most influential queens ever to rule Kemet. She was known as black, beautiful, gorgeous and wise. In fact, this woman from Nubia so captured the heart of the Pharaoh that she changed the course of history.

Tiye was a Nubian princess from birth and married the young Egyptian ruler Amenhotep III. He was so smitten by the beauty and intellect of this woman, that he defied his nations priests and customs by proclaiming the Nubian "commoner" his great Royal Spouse. Amenhotep publicly expressed his love for Queen Tiye, which made her a celebrated and wealthy woman in her own right. He often discussed political and military matters with her and obliged to her counsel. Tiye acted on her title as the Great Royal Wife following the end of her husbands reign. She held "rank" over Kemet during the reign of her three sons and for nearly half a century Tiye governed Kemet. During this time, she regulated her trade and protected her borders. During her time, she was believed to be the standard of beauty, and Amenhotep pronounced that as he treated her in life, so should she be depicted in death-as his equal.

...not just a *SLAVE!*

YAA ASANTEWA- Of the Ashanti Empire

Yaa Asantewa is known for her fight against the British colonialists and is woven throughout the history of Ghana.

One evening the chiefs held a secret meeting at Kumasi. Yaa Asantewa, was the Queen Mother of Ejisu, and was present at this meeting. During the meeting, the chiefs were discussing how they would strategize a war against the white men and force them to bring back the Asantehene (ruler of the Ashanti people). While there, Yaa Asantewa noticed that some of the chiefs looked afraid to pursue. Some proclaimed that there should not be a war and that they should petition the governor to bring back the Asantehene. This greatly irritated and annoyed Yaa Asantewa so much so that she suddenly stood up and spoke. This is what was recorded: "Now I have seen that some of you fear to go forward to fight for our king. If it were in the brave days of Osei Tutu, Okomfo Anokeye, and Opolu Ware, chiefs would not sit down to see their king taken away without firing a shot. No white man could have dared to speak to the chief of the Ashanti in the way the Governor spoke to you chiefs this morning. Is it true that the bravery of the Ashanti is no more? I cannot believe it. It cannot be! I must say this, if you the men of Ashanti will not go forward, then we will. We the women will. I shall call upon my fellow women. We will fight the white men. We will fight til the last of us falls in the battlefields." Following this speech, the men took an oath to fight the white men until they released the Asantehene. Yaa Asantewa led the Ashanti's while bravely fighting and keeping the white men in their forts. The British were losing so badly that they sent in 1,400 soldiers as reinforcement. This led to the capturing of Yaa Asantewa and other leaders. They were all sent into exile. Yaa Asantews's war was the last of the major wars led by a woman in Africa.

...not just a *SLAVE!*

About The Author

Angeline Dean is a sought after speaker and minister. She serves as a committeewoman and is county-co-chair of the Citizen's Campaign. Ms. Dean also hosts her own radio program-Straight Talk, Real Talk, Let's Talk with Angeline Dean. Her company, Dynasty Consulting LLC, not only serves to mentor the youth in her area, but also creates modules that train in such fields as self-esteem, customer service, leadership, and many others.

Ms. Dean finds the core elements that drive her passion are TRUTH and IDENTITY. Thus, her passion for these elements in the field of education. If to educate is to inform, to train, to teach, and to draw out of – then why do we attempt these things without bringing everyone to the table? Presently, she is in a graduate program studying community and economic development, with the hopes of pursuing her Doctorate at Temple University in Multi-Cultural Education.